Faces Hidden in the Dust

FACES HIDDEN IN THE DUST
THE SELECTED GHAZALS OF GHALIB

Translated by
Tony Barnstone and Bilal Shaw

WHITE PINE PRESS / BUFFALO, NEW YORK

White Pine Press
P.O. Box 236
Buffalo, NY 14201
www.whitepine.org

Acknowledgments:
Mayday Magazine (2016): "The Wasteland," "The Tulip," and "Give Me Lunacy at Least." *Kyoto Journal* (2017): "The Idol" and "Seeking a Gash." *Arroyo Literary Review* (2016): "Why?" and "What We Say." *Metamorphoses* (2016): "No Medicine," "Where Is My Heart?", "A Woundgift," and "Who Cares?" *Angle* (2015): "The Hidden Flame." *The Able Muse* (2014): "Out of Heartfire." *Red Wheelbarrow* (2014). "Famine," and "Hennaed Feet." *Askew* (2009): "Enter My Dreams," and "Glances Lines with Kohl."

Grateful acknowledgment goes to the remarkable scholarship of Frances W. Pritchett, whose website "A Desertful of Roses: The Urdu Ghazals of Mirza Asadullah Khan 'GHALIB'" we consulted often. It is a profound and insightful resource for anyone seeking traditional commentary on the ghazals, as well as a deep reading of the puns, wordplay and rhetoric that make Ghalib's work so memorable. Among the many other essential works we consulted, we would especially like to acknowledge Ralph Russell's *The Oxford India Ghalib: Life, Letters and Ghazals*, Natalia Prigarina's *Mirza Ghalib: A Creative Biography*, and K.C. Kanda's *Mirza Ghalib: Selected Lyrics and Letters*.

Publication of this book was supported by a grant from by public funds from the New York State Council on the Arts, with the support of Governor Andrew M. Cuomo and the New York State Legislature, a State Agency and with funds from the Amazon Literary Partnership.

Printed and bound in the United States of America.

Book design: Elaine LaMattina

ISBN 978-1-945680-50-2

Library of Congress Control Number: 2020952146

Table of Contents

Introduction

Ghalib's Life and Times

Mirza Asadullah Beg Khan (1797–1869), known by his pen names Asad ("lion") and Ghalib ("superior"), is the famous romantic and mystical poet of the Mughal Empire (1526–1858) in India. He is the most beloved and most widely-read poet of the Urdu language, the dominant language of northern India and Pakistan that emerged through the blending of Hindustani with Arabic and Persian. He is known for the beautiful prose of his letters and, in fact, brought about a paradigm shift in how letters were written and communicated during his time. His focus on informal yet beautiful writing rather than flowery formal prose was his greatest contribution to the art of Urdu letters. He is also arguably the world's most extraordinary writer of poems in the ghazal form (though certain Persian poets, such as Hafez and Rumi, give him a run for the money).

Ghalib was born in Agra in 1797, in a time of political transition. His lifetime saw the rise of the British colonial empire in India and the concomitant decline of the great Mughal Empire, which had been riven by internal dissent, succession battles, and waves of invasion from Persia, Afghanistan, and the Marathas of the south. Mughal rule was finally eliminated after the 1857 Sepoy Rebellion against the British. Ghalib was the proud descendant of a wealthy, noble, Turkish military family that traced its lineage back to King Tur, the son of Faridun, the legendary Persian king whose rule began with his defeat of the demon king Zahhak, as related in the *Shahnameh,* the Persian *Book of the Kings.*

Ghalib's father died in battle in 1805 when Ghalib was five. The boy's uncle took over raising him but died when Ghalib was seven. After that, his mother's family raised him. He was a brilliant boy who seems to have had an eidetic memory and so, later in life, never got into the practice of buying books. He would borrow them, read them, and have them afterwards permanently available in his mental library. At that early age, he was given a deep education in languages, philosophy, and other subjects, and he began writing poetry in Urdu. His poetry immediately won acclaim—though his highly wrought, witty, allusive, Persianized diction and rhetoric also came in for criticism. Ghalib considered the ghazals he wrote in Persian in his middle period to be his best work (He once remarked: "With the Persian language, I have an amorous relationship."). However, his readers and critics have generally preferred the Urdu ghazals he wrote early and late in life, a selection of which are the poems translated in this book.

His marriage to Umrao Begum, an eleven-year-old girl from a rich and noble Delhi-based family, was arranged in 1810, when he was just thirteen. Marriages were arranged at such an early age with the idea that if you marry children "before the awakening of sexual consciousness" it is more likely that "an orthodox man or woman should never" fall in love with anybody other than their spouse (Snarev, quoted in Prigarina 97). However, this strategy did not work with Ghalib. Upon marriage, Ghalib moved to Delhi, where he was popular as a witty, handsome, tall, and jaunty young man. He is open in his letters about the fact that his marriage was an arrangement, not a union of love, and so, like other noblemen of his day, he looked for love and sex outside of marriage.

Among other affairs suggested in his letters there was one that was a deeply passionate love affair with a Hindu woman who had been hired to sing at his wedding. His lover died tragically and young, and much of his life was spent in mourning this lost, ardent love. Here are some lines from Ghazal 139, "Her Death":

> You said you'd entwine yourself
>   with me for life.
> but even life
>   unravels. O! O!
>
> This water-and-air life
>   is toxic to me
> because it was unhealthy
>   for you. O! O!
>
> What happened to the rose's
>   pride in blooming?
> Red flowers embroider
>   your clay now, O! O!

Shame drove you to hide
    in a veil of dirt.
The veil of love
    has been torn. O! O!

When love's fame
    blended into dirt,
the way of love
    left the planet. O! O!

Some commentators see these last stanzas as indicating that she might have committed suicide because of shame and scandal. Ghalib suggests as much in a letter he writes to a friend in 1860, in which he takes the blame for her death:

> Friend, Mughals are terrible creatures who kill the ones they are dying for. I am also a Mughal. I have loved and cruelly killed a dancing girl...this happened forty or forty-two years ago, but I have not forgotten her entrancing glances.

He mourned his singing woman for the rest of his life, and sought comfort outside of his marriage. It seems clear that he truly did not love his wife. She became increasingly religious in proportion to his lack of faith, and he depicts marriage to her as equivalent to being forced to live in a prison. In his letters, he fantasizes about being single and mourns the "noose of death" that marriage has cast around his neck that on the one hand will not break and on the other hand will not have the mercy to kill him at last (Sadiq 264).

One can imagine that being married to him was equally difficult. As he embarrassedly writes to a friend, "An esteemed sage told me when I was young not to worry too much about asceticism and godliness. Drink, feast, and take joy, but be a fly eating sugar, not a fly stuck in honey." And he quotes to his friend a Persian couplet:

Each spring take a new woman
    into your heart.
Toss last year's woman out
    with your old calendar.

He jokes that even if he were admitted to Paradise and given a virgin *houri* he would be sickened and distressed to have only one companion for all eternity.

Ghalib's marriage also suffered from other tragedies: He had seven children, all of whom died while infants.

Biographies and critical assessments of Ghalib often go into exhaustive detail about his finances because, in fact, his expectations of and lifelong pursuit of financial support from others reveal essential aspects of his character, his family, and of the role of Muslim nobility within the British Empire.

As Ghalib was from a noble (though not a wealthy) family, he didn't have to find himself a profession outside of writing. He was raised to feel entitled to a life of luxury. As P. Hardy notes, Ghalib when young "accepted without difficulty that the British owed him a living as a young relative of Muslim collaborators with the British" colonial enterprise (56), and he studiously avoided the indignity of working for a living so long as he could continue receiving remittances from the British East India Company, and, late in life, from the Mughal ruler.

However, as Sadiq notes,

> The year 1826 came as a turning-point in his life. He had been for some time in straitened circumstances and came to believe that the Nawab had all along withheld part of the pension to which he was entitled as a member of his uncle's family. This led to a prolonged lawsuit which, being decided against him in 1831, left him almost a ruined man. He had acquired expensive habits which his meagre pension... did not enable him to support, and he was involved in serious financial difficulties (242).

He continued to support himself on small remittances from the British government, through the financial help of his friends, and by gambling. In fact, he was jailed for three months in 1847 on charges of running a gambling establishment out of his home.

On his release, he was supported by the Mughal king, who hired him as a poetry tutor and commissioned him in 1850 to write a history of the Mughal Empire. Ghalib the gambler, womanizer, and debtor finally achieved the status, rank, and income he'd been striving for his whole life. But this success was to be short-lived, because the Mughal Empire itself was about to come to an end.

In 1857, the *sepoys*, the Indian troops who swelled the ranks of the British army, enacted a bloody rebellion against the Western occupiers, took over Delhi, and pressured the Mughal King to become their figurehead. The British responded by demolishing the power of the Mughals and putting an end to their rule. During the retaking of the city, British soldiers engaged in looting houses broke into the home of Ghalib's younger brother, Yusuf, and shot him to death. What the British called the Sepoy Rebellion was often termed in India the First War of Indian Independence. The reverberations from this war would spread outward in the future and culminate in India's official independence from the British Empire.

As Sadiq notes, Ghalib had "felt no qualms in transferring his allegiance to the British on learning that the East India Company had decided to terminate the Mughal dynasty on Bahadur Shah's demise," and had in fact written a *qasida* in praise of Queen Victoria, submitting it to Lord Canning "with the request that, as a leading poet, he might be honoured with 'title, robe of honour, and pension'" (Sadiq 245).

But after the Mutiny, Ghalib's difficulties "reached their climax. His pension was withdrawn and for some time he lived precariously by selling his household effects," despite the many *qasidas* he wrote to the British, seeking to flatter them into supporting him again—so many that he was told to stop pestering Lord Canning with his poems (Sadiq 245). It is true that Ghalib "developed a sensitivity to the wrongs and sufferings of his community after the Mutiny," but he subordinated these politics in his quest to receive remittances (245).

As Sadiq dourly puts it, "Ghalib was an opportunist and was not troubled with feelings and sentiments. He held that ideals were for men and not men for ideals, and were on the whole a pretty disagreeable thing if your object was to get on in life" (245). To Ghalib's relief, a few years later he once again began receiving a pension, and was able to live in relative ease for his final years.

Ghalib fell ill in 1862 and began a slow decline in health until his death in 1869—a date remarkable also because it was the year in which Gandhi was born.

If this ugly sketch of Ghalib's marriage and finances leaves you with a sour taste in your mouth, this is as it should be. Despite being generous and loyal to his friends and continuing "to support his servants and dependents even in his darkest days, with his usual cheerfulness and liberality," he had all the faults of the nobility: self-regard, a self-interested subservience to power, a disdain for the "masses" who found his poetry too difficult, a vain relishing of titles and wounded glorification of his noble ancestry in the face of strait-ened circumstances, and a lack of loyalty to his wife of many decades (Sadiq 246-248).

And yet, somehow, this difficult, disreputable, vain man managed to write some of the finest poetry the world has ever seen.

The Religious and Erotic Traditions

The ghazal is known as a form associated with love, but as Ralph Russell succinctly notes, "the love which the ghazal portrays is illicit love…someone else's fiancée or wife or a courtesan or a boy, and in South Asian society, such lovers have faced drastic consequences."

Further, the love might not be a human love, but instead a "love for God or for any ideal in life to which he commits himself absolutely and for which he is prepared, if necessary, to sacrifice his life" (292-293). Thus in many of Ghalib's poems, it is possible to read the lover as male or female or super-natural or all three at once. Traditionally, the lover—God or human—is por-trayed as recalcitrant or forbidden by society, so that the poem becomes an extended moan of unrequited passion.

Though Ghalib's poems fit into this devotional tradition, in truth he was not particularly religious. He broke from his family's Shiite faith, and was more attracted to Shi'a Islam, and even there his devotion was weak—in fact, he was accused of atheism. In a late letter, he writes that he believes in the "oneness of God" and finds atheism "abhorrent"; yet in another of his late letters he writes, "A helpless prisoner of Time, I have little hope from God, not at all from man" and, imagining his own death, "Good riddance! Ghalib has died. An infidel and atheist has died" (Kanda 358). Many of his verses support his attitude of seizing the day instead of delaying pleasure to the afterlife: "Find bliss in partying, wild passion, and a lush life. / Why die of thirst in religion's mirage?" He was a gambler and an adulterer, he broke the prohibition against drinking with a certain degree of relish (in one ghazal he brags, "I pawn my ragged robe and prayer rug for wine"), he never did a pilgrimage to Mecca to see the holy rock of the Ka'aba, and he didn't fast or pray.

Perhaps it is best to think of Ghalib as a freethinking skeptic regarding the ritual practices of formal religion who nonetheless had a spiritual impulse at his core. As he says in one poem, the better religion "discards rituals" because "When creeds are erased, we become one faith." But Sadiq argues that the less skeptical letters are a conventional public face that Ghalib is putting on, and that the skeptical poems reveal his true heart. Certainly, when looking at lines like "I know what paradise really is — / A pleasing illusion to titillate the fancy," and "Let heaven be flung into hell" so that we won't worship God in hopes of reward, Sadiq's argument seems convincing (249-253).

However, the fact that Ghalib spurned most of the precepts of Islam doesn't mean that he didn't worship anything. As he writes in one poem:

> I pray to what is
>   beyond all sense.
> Ka'aba's just a direction in which to pray,
>   those with pure sight say.

If he truly did have a religion, it was the religion of love—the senseless passion that is "beyond all sense." This is why he writes,

I cry Allah!
    with each little word she says.

He's crying out to Allah in pain at his lover's cruelty, but also he's calling his lover Allah, praying to god through praying to love. He makes this even clearer in another poem in which the humble gaze of the worshiper "finds the Ka'aba" in the "canopied elephant litter" that carries his lover.

In the poem "What" he makes it plain that the lover is being put in the position of God and that he is discarding traditional prayer:

I offer my life
    to you.
What is prayer?
    I do not know.

To worship your lover instead of Allah and to pray to her instead of praying towards the Ka'aba is heresy, and Ghalib is a master of manipulating this taboo to accentuate the intensity with which he depicts his passion. His lover is often characterized as an infidel or as an idol that he worships, causing him to fall away from Islam. Perhaps this is an acknowledgment that the great love of his life was a Hindu, or perhaps it is the case that he was never deeply attached to Islam to begin with.

But when trying to nail down Ghalib's poetry with the hammer of biography one is likely to find the instrument too blunt to be effective. His poems often mix identifiable people with traditional and allegorical objects of love. His poems are characterized by an erotic imagery so passionate as to veer at times into madness, and this erotic imagery was also mystical, since Ghalib was writing in a tradition of Indian Bhakti and Persian Sufi poetry that figured the Almighty as the "Beloved," and that figured merging with God as an erotic act.

But such joining with God came with its dangers, as well. Many of the Sufis who sought to join with the Beloved were tortured and murdered by traditional Islamists for their spiritual version of the Muslim faith—and such attacks continue to this day by fundamentalist groups such as ISIS. And so it is that the "mystic lover's love for God necessarily led him into the same dangers as his love for a human beloved did" (Russell 297).

Though Ghalib posits his drinking of wine as a kind of happy breaking of religious precepts, he also references a tradition of Sufi poetry in which the body is a cup made of clay and filled with the wine of the spirit. So when he writes

> I came out of the wine-party
>   so dry inside.
> I promised not to drink,
>   but Cupbearer, couldn't you have tried?

we are to understand the Cupbearer as the one who carries the intoxicating wine of love, which when drunk will cause one to fall in love with Allah. Thus, the Cupbearer can refer to the prophet Muhammad. In fact, veneration of Muhammad is the one area in which Ghalib's poetry is consistently religious. And yet, we also have to understand such passages in the opposite way. After all, his drinking was literal, not figurative. Perhaps in addition to using drinking as a metaphor for religion he is using religion to justify his drinking.

The ancient Indian tradition of religious poetry is well known in the west through the texts of the *Rig Veda*, the *Bhagavad Gita*, and the *Dhammapadda*, but somewhat less known is the deep tradition of erotic poetry in Sanskrit, as exemplified in the poetry of the great playwright Kalidasa, and in the erotic verses of Amaru. Here is Kalidasa, in the "Winter" section of his long poem on "The Seasons," in which the young women who have made love all night long examine their eyes like red lotuses, their lover-bitten lips:

> Knocked out by passion and their bodies' wine
> the lovers sleep with their bodies twined,
> their limbs smelling sweet as the aroma
> of flower wine on their moist lips.

> Lips red with bite marks, and breasts
> scratched and raw from their lovers' nails,

are passionate evidence of the adult pleasures
the young girls tasted last night.

Classical Sanskrit and Prakrit literature is replete with such explicit passages, along with a long tradition in which the poem serves as an erotic joke, or in which sexy passages are presented to the reader, only to be immediately dismissed as morally impure. Consider this poem by Bhartrihari, which begins with a lyrical evocation of womanly beauty worthy of the Song of Songs:

Three waves roll across her waist,
her breasts take flight like wild geese
and her blossoming face is a bright lotus

But the poem concludes with the expected misogynist Buddhist moral:

but a woman is a moody river
where a monster dwells.
Think well before you take that fatal bath.

Ghalib is typically more of a passionate poet who emerges from the Persian ghazal tradition than an erotic poet in the Indian tradition, but there are times when his work seems in line with the Indian erotic tradition sketched above. In "Glances Lined with Kohl," for example, he describes a flower in tight bud whose closed interior is penetrated by a gust:

A private place
    so tight it squeezes out dew.
A gust pierces the folds of a bud, then
    spurts to the face.

Since the spring gust of the poem symbolically represents desire, we quickly understand that the penetration of the bud and its expulsion of liquid is meant to suggest sexual penetration, ecstasy, and orgasm.

When the major tributaries of Indian poetry—the erotic tradition and the tradition of religious poetry—blend, they do so somewhat uneasily, but with extraordinary effect. In the medieval era the purely erotic tradition joins with the religious to create a poetics of mystical eroticism in the devotional poetry of the Bhakti tradition. We can see a similar evolution of the erotic poem in the west, where the Petrarchan tradition of the love sonnet in Raleigh and Shakespeare is transformed in the next century with Herbert and the other Metaphysicals, creating an English religious-erotic tradition.

Bhakti poets such as Mirabai and Chandidas wrote devastatingly beautiful love and sex poems in which the physical joining with the lover was understood as the spiritual joining of the supplicant with the godhead. The loss of self in carnal ecstasy, the pouring over of lover into lover, becomes the prime, recurrent image for connection with the metaphysical.

Here, for example, is a poem by Chandidas written in the voice of Krishna's lover Radha:

> Why tell me what to do?
> Dreaming or awake I see only his black skin.
> I do not even try to fix my tangled hair,
> just pour it in my lap, and wish it were Krishna.
> I call to him, sweet black Krishna, and cry.
> I leave this black hair loosely knotted
> so when my dark love comes to mind
> I can let it down and brood.
> What can I do?
> His black skin is always with me.

and here a poem by the Hindi poet Kabir, whose poetry combines Sufism with Vaishnava devotionalism:

> I've played with other girls but my heart shakes
> as I mount the high stairs to my Master's palace.
> He's to be my lover and I can't be shy.
> My heart must leap toward him. I will lower my veil
>   and touch him with all my body,
> my eyes like ceremonial lamps of love.
> Kabir says, friend, to understand: love. If you do not worship
>   the Lover, why dress up and line your eyes with kohl?

Though the Bhakti tradition was largely a Hindu tradition, in poets such as Kabir we see it joining together with the Sufi tradition of mysticism, and so with it is with Ghalib, who is on the one hand a Muslim poet in the mystical erotic tradition of Rumi and Hafez, but who nonetheless owes a debt to the long Indian tradition of mystical eroticism.

In Ghalib's poems, the lover's faith is most often met with faithlessness, and his love is rewarded with cruelty. In "Give Me Lunacy, at Least," he presents himself as so deeply in love he is willing to accept emotional disaster from his beloved, because at least in that way they still have a connection.

> It is not like
>   I'm giving up faith.
> If love fails, I will take
>   calamity, at least.

In the following stanza the same sentiment is presented, but the lover has now morphed into a cruel God dispensing unjust fate from the heavens:

> Give me a shred,
>   O unjust sky.
> Let me sigh
>   resentfully, at least.

This double strand of the mystical and the erotic creates a strange double-vision experience when reading the poems of Ghalib. In these lines from "Out of Heartfire," for example, Ghalib presents himself as a lover who has been so consumed by love-fire that he has ceased being, and from him like a contagion nonbeing begins to burn up the world and everybody in it:

> The hidden flame is cruel.
>   My heart's burning.
> A whispering ember,
>   the hurt's burning.
> No hunger for her memory
>   eats at my heart.
> There is a firestorm in my house;
>   every part's burning.

I am beyond nonbeing
    and my sighs are hot enough
to make a Phoenix's wings
    start burning.

How do I show the flaming gem
    of my thoughts?
A wild thought kindled in me.
    Now the desert's burning.

The recalcitrant lover who burns one away with desire-fire is a traditional trope for the Beloved of Sufism, in which you must cease to be in order to be entirely, like a drop entering the ocean or a flame eating away the self so that the great spirit can enter and inhabit you where your ego previously resided. So are we reading a poem about love or a poem about God? I think Ghalib would ask, "Is there a difference?"

Ghazals as the Blues

The ghazal form is the most important short poetic form in Arabic, Persian and Urdu poetry, as the sonnet is in English. It is characterized by an initial couplet with a rhyme-repeated phrase combination, followed by a rhyme-repetition in the second line of each succeeding couplet, and a "signature" in which the poet addresses himself in the final line of the poem. This form has become exceedingly popular in English, with many American poets attempting their hand at the form, loosely or strictly, and it is a form often taught in contemporary creative writing workshops. But to understand the ghazals of Ghalib one needs to appreciate not only their formal structure but also how they fit within a social context.

To understand the way the ghazal works with an audience, it helps to know that in Ghalib's day ghazal writers would come together in gatherings where they would perform their poems. As Ralph Russell notes:

An element of competition among them has always been present (especially when, as was often the case in Ghalib's day, the host of the gathering presented beforehand a half-line of verse which had to be incorporated in their own poems by all the poets attending, with both meter and rhyme prescribed for them). (288)

The ghazal, that is, is a spoken form that is often adapted to music, and is only later and secondarily a written art. And—though it might seem at first glance a stretch—a comparison of the ghazal with the blues can help open up the form for the English-language reader.

Ghazals are concerned with many of the same thematic questions that run through the American blues: a distant, uncaring God who makes the poet suffer; a distant, uncaring lover who makes the poet suffer; a lover whom the poet worships like a god; a god whom the poet worships like a lover.

But ghazals also share key structural elements with the blues. In the blues, individual verses typically stand alone instead of building into a coherent, consistent narrative, and yet they share a central theme. Writers of the blues sometimes break this rule, of course. Ghazals are structured in exactly the same fashion.

Ghazal couplets are like modular building blocks out of which the author constructs the house of the song. Thus, a number of Ghalib's ghazals come down to us with alternate arrangements of couplets, or with couplets added or left out. In this way, the ghazal can be seen a collection of short, pithy, stand-alone poems put into a constellation to make a pattern.

Another element of the blues is the repetition of the first line of the verse, followed by another "response line." Thus, in Muddy Waters' "I Got My Mojo Working," the third verse goes:

> I got a gypsy woman givin' me advice
> I got a gypsy woman givin' me advice
> I got some red hot tips I got to keep on ice

The ghazal in written form is in couplet form, but when sung out loud the first line of the couplet is repeated, just as in a blues song. This should change the way you read the ghazal on the page. The second line functions as a response line that completes the action of the first line, but the repetition of the first line elongates your anticipation of—wait for it!—that completed action. In Ghalib's "At This Party," for example, you could read the eighth couplet as a kind of blues verse if you repeated the first line on the page as it is in oral form:

> No, she is not bad,
>   just stubborn.
> No, she is not bad,
>   just stubborn.
> She keeps thousands of promises
>   (when she forgets not to).

or, in the opening couplet of "The Desert Sea":

> Without me weeping,
>   my house would be bleak inside.
> Without me weeping,
>   my house would be bleak inside.
> The sea would be a desert
>   if weren't sea inside.

Blues form has been powerfully adapted by Langston Hughes and others in poetry. Here is the last stanza of Hughes' "Hard Daddy," for example:

> I wish I had wings to
> Fly like de eagle flies.
> Wish I had wings to
> Fly like de eagle flies.
> I'd fly on ma man an'
> I'd scratch out both his eyes.

Note that Hughes likes to emphasize the pause or rhetorical caesura that often splits the blues line into two parts by breaking each line of poetry into two. Ghalib's ghazals have a similar caesura structure, and like Hughes we've chosen to split the couplets in half in order to highlight the wit and rhetoric of the lines.

Laid out on the page in this same way, many of Ghalib's poems could actually be sung as blues songs.

Though Ghalib's poems are written, they emerge from traditions of oral and sung poetry—both the Indian Bhakti tradition and that of the Persian ghazal—in which because poems are often passed down orally from person to person the author's name might be considered a nonessential part of the poem. There is no signature to a song, after all. But in the Bhakti and ghazal tradition there is a signature, in fact: The final couplet of these poems makes reference to the author's name, nickname, or pen name. Thus, Asadullah Khan, known in his early poems by the early pen name Asad and in the later poems as Ghalib, calls out to himself by these names at the end of his poems.

Though the signature line is not generally part of the Blues, it does highlight how deeply the ghazals of Ghalib emerge from an oral and song tradition.

Opening Up the Rhyme

As to the use of rhymes in these translations, our general technique has been to follow the principles I set out in my article "A Manifesto on the Contemporary Sonnet." In that article, I argued that despite the domination of a free verse esthetic in American poetry for the past sixty years, the use of rhyme still makes sense, in part because rhyme makes the poem more memorable (both in the sense of "easy to recall" and in the sense of "remarkable"). As I note there, rhyme makes the poem easier to recall because "rhyme creates an effect of expectation. As in music, knowing that after two lines a rhyming end word will appear helps the sluggish brain to perform." But it also makes the poem more remarkable because "Paradoxically...in the moment of composition this effect of expectation has the effect of introducing the unexpected into the poem. Whatever the topic of the poem, whatever the projected arc of the sentence rhythm and image flow, the rhyme word militates that a random element must enter the poem."

Although we tend to think of rhyme as closing down possibilities in the poem because it gives us the "expected" word, in fact for the acrobatic writer who avoids the easy rhymes (breath and death, fire and desire) it opens the poem up to an almost surreal wildness. The use of rhyme is an experimental technique as wild as anything the avant-garde Oulipo movement came up with (as in their N+7 technique in which you substitute for each noun the noun that follows it by seven entries in a dictionary).

Advertising, songwriting, and millennia of poetry, however, have caused many of the best rhymes to be exhausted, and so the time is ripe for the technique of rhyme to be opened up to wildness again. Thus, I recommend the use of slant rhymes (assonance, consonance, and full consonance), sight rhymes (words that are spelled like rhymes but that are unrhymed when pronounced), repetition rhymes (repetition instead of rhyme), inclusion rhymes (words that include the rhyme word), and homograph rhymes (words spelled the same but sounding different, like "dove" the bird and "dove" the action).

In translation, in particular, this opening up of rhyme is a vital technique. The translator who wishes to maintain the form of the original in the poem in English has many fewer choices than the original poet has. After all, the poet can choose rhymes first and write lines to fill in the poem. The translator, on the other hand, is working from already-written lines and needs to stay close to the letter and spirit of those lines while simultaneously injecting rhymes into the poem. The problem when translating Ghalib is particularly dire, because the translator must maintain both the rhyme and the repetend (the repeated word). That doesn't merely double the difficulty; it multiplies it exponentially.

Despite this difficulty, Bilal and I have maintained true rhyme and repetition in a minority of these poems, as in "Out of Heartfire":

> How awful to see Heaven's teeth
>   circling the finger
> of you who deserve pearls
>   to string your finger.
>
> My souvenir of you
>   is that you didn't give me one.
> The day you left me
>   you raised a ringless finger.

Asad, when I write hot words
    out of heartfire
no one dares give
    the words I sing the finger.

We did so as well in "Call Down Lightning":

All I do is take my ease;
    they're right to sneer at me.
In my hometown,
    dawn's teeth leer at me.

My soul hunts a singer
    with fiery breath
whose voice calls lightning
    down to sear me.

I wander the delirious valley
    of my thoughts
'til no desire to return
    appears to me.

You unveil lewdly
    in the garden.
I blush when roses
    scent the air near me.

How could my secret heart
    be known?
My own poems
    smear me.

However, these and other poems in the book are exceptions that prove the rule: generally speaking, too much of the essence of the poem is lost through the use of true rhyme and true repetition to make the practice of worth for the translator who wishes to make his or her translations poetry in English. Even if the poem evades the Devil and the deep blue sea of padding and inaccuracy, there is still the deep injury that comes with the loss of the essential characteristic of Ghalib's poems: their wit.

True, the rhyme + repetend combination at the end of the couplet is an essential part of the wit and rhetoric of ghazal, but we have chosen instead to highlight other aspects of wordplay, wit and rhetoric in these poems and to loosen the rhyme and repetition in order to keep the poems pithy and elegant instead of uncomfortably pretzeled into shape.

Needless to say, it is easier to maintain true rhyme and repetition in shorter ghazals than in longer ones! More often, we chose to open up the rhymes through use of the techniques enumerated above. In Ghazal 232, for example, we vary true rhyme with the use of homonym rhyme (wine + whine) and sight rhyme (wine+routine) and in Ghazal 31, we used the slant rhyme technique of assonance instead of true rhymes so as to stay as close to the original as possible (bleak/sea/squeeze/free).

These innovations are not merely the product of the translators' limitations; at times Ghalib himself uses similar techniques. In "Then," for example, Ghalib uses repetition instead of rhyme to conclude the first two stanzas:

> I wept so much,
>   love made me bolder then.
> I was washed so clean,
>   I was purer then.
>
> I sold my wine utensils
>   to buy more wine.
> If this were my one arithmetic,
>   I'd be purer then.

And in "The Spell of Desire," he uses no repetitions, but instead uses just rhymes, and we have followed suit in our English version:

> The spell of desire fails,
>   so let me pray instead
> that Khizr the Immortal
>   not be dead.

Do not wander absurdly lost
   in the heat-mirage of being.
Now you have depths and skies
   inside your head.

The spectacle of union is my fantasy,
   but what fancy
will polish the dirty mirror
   where anticipation is read?

Each single atom of the lover
   worships the sun.
Now I am only dust in the air
   but my lust for her sun has not fled.

Ghalib, do not ask how large
   is the wine-house of madness.
The bowl of sky shrinks
   to a dustbin overhead.

The Problem with Repetends

Though repeating a word or phrase can seem, well, repetitive, to readers coming to the poem on the page, it is essential to the ghazal as performance. It "makes an enormous appeal to the audience" at a ghazal-recital gathering, "for quite often they can see what the ending of the second line of the couplet will be and will recite it along with the poet" (Russell 289).

However, often the repeating word in Urdu does not lend itself to English translation, because it is a word such as "is," which rarely appears at the end of English sentences and which if maintained as the repeated word in translation would make the poems read as stilted and artificial. Thus, in the cases in which we chose to maintain the rhyme-repetition form we frequently chose a different word to be the repetend.

Even so, to maintain the form in English without adding in elements foreign to the poem and without padding out the lines and making them clumsy was extraordinarily difficult. One solution we came up with was to allow for the repeated word to vary at times into something like a repetend's equivalent of "slant rhyme." In our English version of Ghazal 17, for example, the repeating word is "her" and the rhyme word is "full." Although we did our best to maintain the rhyme and repetition all the way through the poem, we chose to open up the rhyme, to allow slant rhyme (full/girl) as well as true rhyme (full/particle), and we similarly opened up the repeating word to wordplay (her/here). "Here" is a word that includes the word "Her," and though the vowel changes from a soft "e" to a hard one, it largely sounds the same because of the full consonance.

We used a similar technique in Ghazal 27, where the rhyme word is "high" and the repeating word we chose is "sea" (in the original, the repeating word is "the," but, of course, in English it is hard to end a sentence on that word!) Here we sought out homonyms—that is words that are spelled differently but which sound the same. Thus "high" and "sea" are paired with "eye" and "see." In Ghazal 117 we used the same technique: "icy" repeats with the homonyms "eye sees" and "high seas" and in the last line with the slant rhyme "obscene."

> When my heart sees a hot scene
> jealousy makes it icy.
> My wince cracks wide open
> with what the eye sees.

> The joy of sin should be strong
> as my heart hunger.
> My hemline soaks up
> seven high seas.

> Each handful of dust in the garden
> croons like a turtledove,
> because she's tall as a cypress,
> and her strut's a mite obscene.

Many times, to be both accurate and to bring across the wit, we have included a repeated word but have allowed it to appear anywhere in the line—a bit like internal rhyme, but instead internal repetition.

Overall, we have chosen to choose our battles in these translations. We have generally avoided meter and instead have sought to bring across English equivalents for other aspects of the Urdu form: rhyme, repetition, rhetoric, puns, and wordplay.

Rhetorical Play and Wit

Ghalib is a major poet largely because his poems are among the wittiest the world has ever seen. In this book, we've sought more than anything to replicate this wit, or at least to come up with equivalent wordplay and rhetorical fun in the English translation of his couplets.

Masters of wit in English language verse often structure the couplet via parallelism and reverse parallelism, as in the opening of "To Dorothy" by contemporary poet Marvin Bell:

> You are not beautiful exactly.
> You are beautiful, inexactly.

A similar structure can be seen in Ghalib's "The Betel Nut":

> They say people live
>   on hope.
> I do not even hope
>   to live.

But in the Ghalib example, the complex play of parallelism and reversal also inverts the order of the parallel phrases (the classical Greek rhetorical term for this would be *chiasmus* or *antimetabole*).

Whereas parallelism creates a sense of pleasant repetition and keen phrasing, reverse parallelism is more likely to create the effect of betrayal of expectation that is at the core of most if not all humor.

This betrayal of expectation can be created in many ways, of course, but the couplet structure is uniquely suited to it. We often talk about funny quips as "one-liners," but even within the one-liner there is an implicit pause between the setup and the punchline of the joke. Here, for example is a Stephen Wright one-liner: "I saw a bank that said '24 Hour Banking,' but I do not have that much time." The joke would work even better if the "wait-for-it" pause before the punchline were emphasized by a line break:

> I saw a bank that said "24 Hour Banking,"
> but I do not have that much time

Here are some other one-liners turned into couplets:

> I couldn't figure out why the ball kept getting bigger and bigger.
> And then it hit me.
> —Anonymous

> A woman without a man
> is like a fish without a bicycle
> —Gloria Steinem

The one-liner's structure can often be seen as energizing the heroic couplet with humor and wit, as in these lines from Alexander Pope's poem "Couplets On Wit":

> Now wits gain praise by copying other wits
> As one Hog lives on what another shits.

Ghalib's couplets are often funny and wry like these one liners:

> Ghalib, why is a preacher
>   like a tavern door?
> Bear in mind, yesterday
>   I came out and he swung in!

My wasteland
    is such a wasteland
that seeing the desert,
    I recall home.

But Ghalib is not always funny, ironic, sarcastic, biting in his wit. He is also cherished for his remarkable imagery, which often veers into the surreal when dealing with ecstatic religious or erotic states:

Do not ask about mirage waves
    in the desert of faith.
A sword edge shines
    in each sand particle here.

Though he often uses *chiasmus* or the one-liner structure detailed above, the wit in Ghalib's poems is wildly inventive, hard to categorize, often blending these techniques with wordplay, puns, and ironic metaphor, as in these lines from "The Jewel of the Party":

I act indifferent,
    a veil draped over secret lust.
But I am lost to her.
    She finds me out.

A good example of how complex his punning can get can be found in these lines from "Seeking a Gash," where the lover's dark hair tosses the whole world into darkness, tangling us up in its curls:

Again the world is tangled
    in darkness
by the cruel rulings
    of her unruly hair.

In the Urdu, also, there is a wordplay where the curls are described as *sarish-tah-daarii*, where *sarishtah* alone means "rope" or "cord" or "rites" or "office of records," but when combined with *daarii* refers to a scribe and petition-presenter in a court. The wordplay thus suggests that the tyrannical hair tangles the world in dark and twisted court rulings. Clearly, the exact wordplay is not translatable, but in "the cruel rulings of her unruly hair" we've sought to create a bit of equivalent cleverness, on the theory that in lines such as these the wordplay is the spirit that makes the language poetry. Without that animating poetic spirit, all that is left is the profane flesh of words.

Questions of being and nothingness are at the core of many of Ghalib's wittiest poems. Here is his poem "No One," for example:

> Let me live somewhere
> 　good with no one,
> speaking and being
> 　understood by no one.
>
> I'd like to build a door-less,
> 　wall-less house
> with no guard, here in the
> 　neighborhood of no one.
>
> Then when I fall sick
> 　no one will be my healer.
> My death song will be sung the way
> 　it should—by no one.

The wordplay and humor are reminiscent of the famous Bert Williams song, "Nobody":

> I ain't never done nothin' to nobody
> I ain't never got nothin' from nobody, no time
> And until I get somethin' from somebody, sometime
> I will never do nothin' for nobody, no time

In Ghalib's case, though, the wit is used to highlight the troubles he has connecting with his lover (and his God). It can also be used as a way of understanding the paradoxes of being and nonbeing from a spiritual perspective. The Sufi notion is that in order to merge with the great spirit, the Beloved, one must first annihilate the self.

Ghalib's poem "Nothing" continues the spiritual meditation on being and nothingness through an allusion to the famous hymn from the *Rig Veda* on "The Creation." In this veda, as in many creation myths from around the world, the poet strives to imagine what was before anything was, what existed before existence existed:

> Before being, before even nonbeing,
> there was no air, no firmament.
> So, what breathed? And where? And by whose order?
> And was there water endlessly deep?
> This was before death or immortality.
> There was no division between night and day,
> yet instinctively there was breathing,
> windless breathing and nothing else,
> so dark that darkness was hidden in the dark.

Ghalib's "Nothing" launches a similar metaphysical investigation:

> Before being there was God.
>   If nothing were, God still would be.
> Being drowns me.
>   What matter if I have no being?

Our primary translating task in this book has been to create a Ghalib whose poems are as witty in English as in the original. It isn't always or even often possible to translate puns and wordplays from language to language. Idiomatic expressions and connotative levels are far too different to allow the translator to effectively translate both surface and depth. Therefore, we have striven to use Ghalib's techniques in English to create puns, jokes, and wordplays that are similar to the original, if not the same. More, we've taken every opportunity to create wordplays in English, with the idea that such moments of wit can make up for other moments where we were unable to bring Ghalib's wit across elegantly, concisely, and effectively and so chose to focus instead on the level of primary meaning, as in "Her shyness makes her shy away / in shame," or:

The desire to grow faith
  withers in my heart.
What remains is remains
  of desire to desire.

Ghalib loves to use paradox to suggest heartbreak ironies, but also to suggest distance from Allah and the desire for spiritual connection. The paradox, like the joke, is designed to set up a frame of meaning and then to knock it down. The effect of this can be humorous or it can be revelatory, or both, and it is a standard trick in spiritual texts around the world.

Such paradoxes can be seen in the stanza above from "Pawned to This Cruel Life." Here, much of the wordplay in the original has to do with a farming metaphor in which the desire to cultivate faith has been erased from a farmer's heart because no harvest except grief for the harvest remains. In our version, we sought to bring the meaning across and to echo the repetition of key terms in the original, but also to take the opportunity to pun on the word "remains," which in addition to its meaning of "is left" as a verb can also mean "corpse" as a noun. Though that exact pun does not exist in the original, the lines are filled with equivalent puns that also meditate on growth and death, creation and absence, faith and faithlessness. Thus, like Marvin Bell, we strive not to be "beautiful exactly," but to be "beautiful inexactly."

May you enjoy the exactingly inexact beauty of these translations.

—Tony Barnstone
Whittier College, 2021

Works Cited

Hardy, P. "Ghalib and the British." In Ralph Russell, ed. Ghalib: *The Poet and His Age*, pp. 54-69. George Allen & Unwin. Cambridge: 1972.

Kanda, K.C. *Mirza Ghalib: Selected Letters and Lyrics*. New Dawn Press. SA, UK, India: 2004.

Russell, Ralph, ed. *The Oxford India Ghalib*. Oxford University Press. New Delhi, New York, London: 2003.

Prigarina, Natalia. *Mirza Ghalib: A Creative Biography*. Translated from the Russian by M. Osama Faruqi. Oxford, New York: 2000.

Sadiq, Muhammad. *A History of Urdu Literature*. Oxford University Press. Oxford: 1984, first edition 1964.

Snarev, A.E. *Ethnographic India*. Moscow, 1981. (Russian)

The Poems

The Hidden Flame

The hidden flame is cruel.
   My heart's burning.
A whispering ember,
   the hurt's burning.

No hunger for her memory
   eats at my heart.
There is a firestorm in my house;
   every part's burning.

I am beyond nonbeing
   and my sighs are hot enough
to make a Phoenix's wings
   start burning.

How do I show the flaming gem
   of my thoughts?
A wild thought kindled in me
   and set the desert burning.

I have no heart
   or I'd show you my flower wounds.
How can I put on a fireworks show
   when my shirt's burning?

Ghalib, it's come down to me
   and a thirst for ice, for my heart
took people's false warmth to heart
   and started burning.

(Ghazal 5)

41

Out of Heartfire

How awful to see Heaven's teeth
   ringing your finger.
You deserve pearls
   encircling your finger.

My keepsake of you
   is that you didn't give me one.
The day you left me
   you raised a ringless finger.

Asad, when I write searing words
   out of heart-fire
no one dares give
   the words I sing the finger.

(Ghazal 50)

The Jewel of the Party

Look at this fate.
   I'm even jealous of myself.
Do I dare look at her?
    Look, I just cannot do it.

Wash the heart off your hands
   when suspicion burns.
Suspicion swirls like wine
   and melts the wineglass.

O God, how can she tell that man,
   "Behave yourself?"
Her shyness makes her shy away
   in shame.

Lust has its way.
   It makes each breath a groan.
My heart is so spooked,
   it is afraid to breathe.

Bravo! What a party!
   Go away, evil eye.
Even my wailing
   turns into a song here.

I act indifferent
   and throw a veil over my secret lust.
I am lost to her,
   but she finds me out.

I heard you say,
   "He's the jewel of the party."
His impression sank into you.
   My heart sank, too.

That fairy-faced girl
    is more ethereal when in love.
Her color blossoms
    as it wanes.

Even her portrait flirts
    with the artist.
The more he draws,
    the more he is drawn.

Asad, your shadow flees from you
    like smoke.
Your soul is fire.
    Nothing can stand this heat.

(Ghazal 153)

At This Party

At this party it is useless
   to be modest.
All I do is sit here,
   yet fingers point at me.

It is just a heart,
   scared of the doorman's power.
I walk past your door,
   but do not speak.

I pawn my ragged robe
   and prayer rug for wine.
It has been too long since I feasted
   on wind and dew.

Even at immortal Khizr's age,
   my life would still be waste.
Tomorrow he will ask you, too,
   "What did you do?"

If I could interrogate the dust,
   I'd ask, "O Miser!
What did you do
   with the treasure you hoarded?"

On which day does the enemy
   not slice me with slander?
Which day does not see
   the blade saw my head?

I hope she did not learn
   this new habit from him
—she kisses you even
   before you beg.

No, she is not bad,
    just stubborn.
She keeps thousands of promises
    when she forgets not to.

Ghalib, ask yourself,
    do you really expect an answer?
Yet you keep talking
    so long as she'll listen.

(Ghazal 151)

The Spell of Desire

The spell of desire fails,
    so let me pray instead
that Khizr the Immortal
    is not dead.

Do not wander absurdly lost
    in the heat-mirage of being.
Now you have depths and skies
    inside your head.

The spectacle of union is my fantasy,
    but what fancy
will polish the dirty mirror
    where anticipation is read?

Each single atom of the lover
    worships the sun.
I'm gone like dust on the wind,
    but my lust for her sun has not sped.

Ghalib, do not ask how large
    is the wine-house of madness.
The bowl of sky shrinks
    to a dustbin overhead.

(Ghazal 68)

Murderess

Let Jesus be the son of Mary.
    I could not care less
—unless he can cure
    my distress.

Sharia and the Constitution
    bind us,
but what can you do
    with such a murderess?

Her walk is a shot
    from a taut bow.
How can my arrow pierce the heart
    behind her hard breast?

I say one word.
    She cuts off my tongue.
What can I say?
    She says, "Listen," and I say, "Yes?"

Listen to me drivel
    in delirium.
God, what can I mean?
    I hope no one can guess.

If someone slanders,
    why listen?
If someone acts nasty,
    why protest?

You can stop someone
    from walking the dark path.
You can pity
    those who transgress.

Who is there
   who is not in need?
Who can really fill
   anyone's emptiness?

Look how Khizr
   abandoned Alexander.
Now who can guide
   my progress?

Ghalib, what is the use
   of whining
when even hope
   has left?

(Ghazal 215)

Executioner

It is like this:
    her gestures suggest another.
When she loves me,
    I suspect an other.

O God, they have not and will never
    understand my words.
Give another heart to those
    who will not give me their tongue.

Was that coy glance
    shot from the eyebrow?
It is an arrow,
    but from another bow.

When you are in the city,
    I do not wake in grief.
I go to the bazaar and buy
    another heart and life.

How skilled we have become
    at smashing idols!
Yet in our road
    there is another boulder.

My liver-blood seethes.
    I would weep my heart raw
if I had another set
    of pure blood-splashing eyes.

I would die to hear her voice.
    Let my head fly off!
Let her tell the executioner,
    "Yes, another!"

People think the sun
   turns the world to char.
Each day I reveal
   another hidden scar.

I would take (if I did not give
   my heart) peace.
I would breathe (if I did not die
   that day) another sigh.

Grief floods
   when it does not find a channel.
My dammed feelings
   flow another way.

There are other great poets
   in this world,
but Ghalib's style
   is from another world!

(*Ghazal 62*)

The Idol

Of course my idol
   is more than life to me.
Isn't faith
   like my life to me?

It poked from my heart,
   but did not leave the heart.
The tip of your arrow
   is life to me.

Wait. Be strong.
   Only then will things change, Ghalib.
It is hard to live with,
   but life is life to me.

(Ghazal 70)

A Direction in Which to Pray

Being faithful to me is betrayal,
    your lover would say.
The good are always called bad,
    I heard them say.

Today I will share
    my unquiet heart with her.
I am on my way to see
    what I am spurred to say.

Do not talk to them.
    They are old, out of touch.
They say wine and song will relieve me.
    Absurd, I say.

You invade my heart
    when I wake up from fainting.
So why complain?
    I prefer this way.

I pray to what is
    beyond sense.
Ka'aba's merely a direction to face in prayer,
    those with pure-sight say.

Now that you have shown mercy
    to my wounded feet,
thorns on the path to you
    are soothing herbs, I say.

Why be afraid?
    There is a spark in my heart.
They say I need air. They are wrong.
    I need to burn, I say.

Let us see what colors
    her hauteur brings out.
I cry, "Allah!"
    at each tiny word she says.

Now let poets Vehshat and Shefta
    recite elegies.
Ghalib, singer of sad songs,
    is dead and interred, I say.

(Ghazal 86)

What Comes

Not one of my hopes
   comes true.
I cannot see a road
   to come.

My death day
   is already fixed,
so why will night-sleep
   not come?

I used to laugh
   at my heart.
Now, no laugh
   will come.

I know faith and piety
   are rewarded,
but they do not come
   to me.

There is a reason
   why I am silent.
Come on.
   Do you think I am dumb?

Remember when
   I was screaming?
You hear me only
   when silence comes.

The invisible burn scar
   on my heart,
O Savior, does its stench
   not come to you?

I am in a place
    from which
even my own news
    does not come to me.

I die in the desire
    to die.
Death comes but does not
    come to me.

What face will you take
    to the Ka'aba, Ghalib?
Come on, don't you have
    any shame?

(Ghazal 161)

Seeking a Gash

My heart is
   uneasy again.
My chest seeks
   a gash.

Again fingernails dig
   into my liver.
Time to harvest
   bloody tulips.

Again my humble-gaze finds
   Ka'aba
in the curtain of your canopied
   elephant-litter.

Again my brokering eyes hunt
   objects of disgrace.
My shopping heart buys a taste
   of misery.

Again that lamentation
   in a hundred colors.
Again this sweating tears
   in a hundred ways.

Again my collected heart
   is blown about as she breezes by.
It is the whirlwind
   of the apocalypse.

Again your beauty
   parades coquetry.
Today is bazaar day.
   I sell my life.

Again I die
   because of that tramp.
Again this dying is
   my life.

Again court doors crack open
   to her flirting,
and criminal trials
   are hot.

Again the world is tangled
   in darkness
by the cruel rulings
   of her unruly hair.

Again, pieces of my liver
   submit complaints
in one great
   sob.

Again the witnesses
   to love are subpoenaed.
An order is issued:
   "Sweat tears!"

A lawsuit between
   heart and eyelashes.
Today again
   they face a hearing.

Ghalib, to lose your self
   is a gain.
There is something behind
   that veil.

Ghazal 164

Enough

My thin heart cannot eat this grief
    of mine enough.
My sorrow is full because there is not
    rose wine enough.

I am ashamed to tell
    the Cupbearer
I will drink even sediment
    if it is fine enough.

There is no arrow in the bow,
    no hunter in ambush.
In the corner of this cage,
    I can recline enough.

How I revere abstinence!
    Am I a hypocrite?
I half thirst for a reward
    for being dry enough.

How proud the smart ones are.
    They take the road not taken.
But ritual ways bind their feet
    and are routine enough.

Leave me at Zamzam.
    Why should I want to circle the Ka'aba?
My pilgrim robe is soaked
    with wine enough.

It will torture me if things
    do not work out
now that she has given in.
    I guess I whined enough.

O death, my liver is not yet blood
   dripping from my eyes.
I have things to do!
   Give me time enough.

Could there be someone
   who does not know Ghalib?
He is notorious, but as a poet
   he is divine enough.

(Ghazal 232)

Enter My Dream

When you enter my dream
    my restlessness can rest.
But my kinetic heart is too frenetic
    to let me dream.

Your tears of affection
    murder me.
Only you can quench the hot sword
    of your glance.

Your lips quiver.
    Oh, just finish me off.
If you will not kiss,
    use your mouth to answer.

Cupbearer, if you hate me, let me drink
    from your cupped palms.
If you have no cup, do not give it.
    But give me wine.

Asad, your hands and legs
    swell with happiness
when she says, "Give me
    a foot-massage, please."

(Ghazal 193)

Thirst

I came out of the wine party
    dry inside.
I promised not to drink,
    but Cupbearer, couldn't you have tried?

My lover is an arrow
    skewering my heart and liver.
They once were two,
    but now they are unified.

Can you impress me
    by untangling this sorrow, Ghalib?
Your nails solved love knots
    when you had none to untie.

(Ghazal 30)

A Smaller Miracle

With every word, you taunt,
   "What are you?"
You tell me.
   What makes you talk like that?

Flame is a smaller miracle.
   Lightning flirts less than she.
Can someone tell me
   what to make of her angry flirting?

I am so jealous of the man
   you chat with,
I do not panic about
   what my enemy teaches you.

The robe sticks to my body
   with blood,
so what good is it
   to sew the torn collar?

Where the body is charred,
   the heart must be char, too.
You claw the ashes.
   What do you expect to find?

I do not believe in
   what sprints through veins.
Until it drips from my eyes,
   what is blood?

Paradise has something
   precious to us,
but what? Nothing
   but musky rose-blush wine.

Only drink wine
    when you see a few casks.
What are these glasses and bowls
    and goblets and flasks?

My voice is weak,
    but even if I could speak
with what hope could I ask,
    "What do you desire?"

Now that he is the Shah's favorite,
    he puts on airs.
Otherwise, what honor
    does Ghalib have in this town?

(Ghazal 178)

Wine Wave

Again it is time to open wings
    on a wine wave
and give the wine duck a heart
    and swimming hands on a wine wave.

Do not ask why the lords
    are black drunk in the garden.
In the shadow of the grapevine
    the air rides on a wine wave.

He is sunk under wine,
    but it is a good fate.
Huma's wing passes overhead
    in a wine wave.

The monsoon is a season
    when it is not strange
for a sexual breeze to turn
    a life wave into a wine wave.

Four storms rise from
    an emotional whirlwind:
rosewhirl, duskwhirl,
    windwhirl, winewhirl.

The vegetable soul's liver
    thirsts to flower proudly,
and find peace in this water of life,
    in this wine wave.

It courses like blood
    through the grapevine vein
with a royal feather of color opening wings:
    this wine wave.

The rose wave lamplights
    the pathway of thought.
It spills brilliance in imagination,
    the wine wave.

Behind a veil of drunkenness,
    it bathes the toy-show mind,
but still keeps its head
    and flourishes, this wine wave.

This season's typhoon moods
    are so high,
they toss new waves
    of green in a wine wave.

It shows the disturbance of being
    —praise the season of roses.
It guides the drop to the sea
    —praise the wine wave.

Seeing the glorious roses,
    Asad's mind soars.
It is spring, time to spread
    wings of a wine wave.

(Ghazal 49)

Stay Drunk

At my wine party,
   unfold to me one day,
or I will get sloshed
   and tease you free, one day.

Why be proud at the zenith
   of the world's basement?
To fall low
   is height's destiny, one day.

I borrow money to stay drunk,
   thinking for sure
my feast of thirst
   will color me pleased, one day.

O heart, even grief songs
   are blessings,
since the life song
   will cease, one day.

She is a flirt from veil to shoe
   and this dust-up is not her style,
Ghalib! I beat her to it
   so she beat me, one day.

(Ghazal 90)

The Empty Cup

Do not breathe one breath
   that does not pull in desire.
No wine? Then pull on the empty cup
   with oceanic patience.

Don't ask about the purefire
   of my visionquest.
Do pull polished lines from my mirror
   like thorns.

To you, waiting is a pretense
   to untense, O heart!
Who said you could pull off
   being a deadbeat?

He is Narcissus
   ogling you.
My rival has a blind heart and eye,
   so pull wine from your cup.

Pay off your flirtation
   with a coy slash of a glance.
Pull the secret dagger
   from its sheath in my liver.

My glass holds
   the wine of hidden fire.
For my dinner, pull out
   the salamander-heart kebabs.

(Ghazal 56)

A Stunned Drop of Wine

Holding its breath:
   a stunned drop of wine.
Pearls are strung
   along a line of wine.

My heart was flattened because
   the wrecking ball knew I loved her.
She blames me
   even when he mews and whines.

(Ghazal 28)

Then

I wept so much,
    love made me bolder then.
I was washed so clean,
    I was purer then.

I sold my wine utensils
    to buy more wine.
If this were my only math,
    I'd be purer then.

Your vagrancy
    made you infamous
among all the people
    you were smarter than.

Who says nothing occurred
    when the nightingale sobbed?
Behind the rose's veil, a hundred thousand
    livers were slivered then.

Why ask, "Did the man and his flame
    exist or not?"
The lovers were kindling
    of their own fire then.

I went to complain
    about her indifference.
With a glance
    she turned me to dirt then.

Yesterday she lifted Asad's bier
    rudely.
Even his enemies were downcast
    at what they saw in her then.

(Ghazal 210)

The Betel Nut

I am not hopeless
    that love will bear fruit:
Life is a betel nut, not
    a willow tree.

Sultanates pass
    from hand to hand.
This wineglass is not
    Jamshid's signet ring.

Your light sparks
    our being.
Without a sunray there is no
    sand grain.

Do not let out
    the lover's notorious secret
or death will cease
    being mystery.

We fear joy's color
    will orbit off.
A grief-deprived life is not
    lifelong.

They say people live
    on hope.
I do not even hope
    to live.

(Ghazal 95)

My Desires Are Legion

I have thousands of passions.
    Each is too much to bear.
The more they come true
    the less they bear fruit.

Why should my killer
    fear blame will stain her?
My eyes always gush blood.
    I bear it with each breath.

We always hear how Adam
    was cast from the garden.
From your street I emerge,
    bearing more disgrace.

Cruel one, your uprightness
    is a tall tale revealed
when you bare your curls
    and let down your hair.

If you want a letter written,
    let it be by me.
I leave my house, a pen behind my ear,
    and dawn is born.

I hoped
    she would heal my wounds,
but she bears a wound worse than mine
    from his tyrannical sword.

Love makes life
    the same as death.
I am born when I see that pagan;
    without her I cannot breathe.

These days, people equate
    wine drinking with me.
It is time for Jamshid's Cup
    to be reborn in the world.

Ghalib, why is a preacher
    like a tavern door?
Bear in mind, yesterday
    I came out and he swung in!

(Ghazal 219)

The Sound of My Own Failure

I am not the flower of song
　　nor the fretted chord.
I am the sound
　　of my own failure.

You worry, how curly
　　is my black hair?
I worry about the far
　　future.

Your boast of wisdom
　　fools your simple heart
but your breast melts
　　with secret fire.

I am netted
　　in the bird-catcher's love.
Released, I would be
　　tough enough to soar.

If only one day
　　she would flirt with me.
Instead, I long for her
　　torture.

My playful eyelashes
　　flower-toss
each drop of heart blood
　　that spurts.

O your sidelong glance
　　turns me on.
O your cruelty
　　is all style and figure.

You magically appear.
    Congratulations!
I grovel, forehead to the ground
    in prayer.

If you ask me, "Is it so bad?"
    I will say,
"Yes, I am poor.
    But at least you care for the poor."

O Asadullah Khan,
    you are done for.
Oh, hell,
    you alcoholic whoremonger!

(Ghazal 71)

The Accounting

For every drop spilled,
    I must account in full to her.
She lends me lover's eyelashes.
    My liver blood is collateral for her.

Here I am, moaning
    for a cityful of desires.
She splinters the mirror.
    It holds pictures — all of her.

Drag my bier
    through the alleys because
I would die on the road,
    enthralled by her.

Do not ask about mirage waves
    in the desert of faith.
A sword edge shines
    in each sand particle here.

I knew little of love grief
    but life grief
waxes as I recover
    from loving a girl like her.

(Ghazal 16)

Deadbeat Heart

Wash your hands of income,
    O outgoing passion!
Wild tears flow till debt
    drowns the deadbeat heart.

Like a guttering
    candle,
among the seared ones
    I am not utterly burnt out.

(Ghazal 137)

Pawned to This Cruel Life

I would appeal to you
    but I remain unfit.
The heart I was proud of
    has no heart to remain.

I leave, carrying the scar
    of life lust.
I remain, a candle snuffed, unworthy
    of the congregation.

O heart, find a new way
    to die.
No, I remain, not even worth
    the dagger in a murderer's hand.

Facing six directions,
    the mirror door opens.
No split between perfect
    and imperfect remains.

Passion has untied the ties
    of beauty's veil.
To stop me now nothing remains
    — except her gaze.

Though I remain pawned
    to this nasty life,
I do not remain dead
    to the thought of you.

The desire to grow faith
    withers in my heart.
What remains is remains
    of desire to desire.

I do not fear the tyranny of passion,
    but perhaps, Asad,
the heart I was proud of
    has no heart to remain.

(Ghazal 41)

She Pawned Her Heart

She pawned her heart.
   Now she must sit alone.
My loneliness has paid off:
   now they praise me.

The cosmos formed of elements
   wants decay.
The sun is guttering in its sphere,
   a lamp in the windy street.

(Ghazal 105)

The Dead Lamp

You are cruel. Have mercy.
    I am guttering like a snuffed lamp.
I am sick with faith and my pulse is smoke
    fluttering in a snuffed lamp.

I burn to link
    my heart with yours.
Otherwise, my reward is
    an utterly snuffed lamp.

(Ghazal 146)

Everything Will Be Dust

She is pure until my heart lusts
    for death.
But I am a coward.
    The dagger is back in the murderer's palm.

When she speaks
    it is sensual
and my heart speaks,
    so to speak.

This mockery of me
    is luckier than me
since it is presented
    in her presence.

Swarming despair, let me be!
    Everything will be dust,
even delicious futility,
    my last pleasure.

Why draw a road of sorrow?
    I love dragging my feet.
My footstep is in the path.
    I cannot lift it.

True, my heart is a miracle
    of hell flame,
but are your tantrums
    the Apocalypse?

Ghalib's crazy heart
    is spellbound and knotted.
Have pity on longing.
    It belongs to you!

(Ghazal 157)

Red Flowers Hidden in Dust

Some of them came back
   as red flowers.
What faces came, surfacing
   in the dust?

The party decorations
   I recalled in color
become knick-knacks
   in the icon niche of memory.

The Daughters of the Dead
   are veiled in daylight.
What are they thinking?
   At night, they come out naked.

In prison Jacob hears
   no news of Joseph
but his eyes become
   chinks in his cell-wall.

Rivals make lovers unhappy,
   but when Joseph, Moon of Canaan,
moonstruck the Egyptian women,
   Zulaikha became happy.

In this night of separation,
   let my eyes drip a blood river
like two candles
   becoming fire.

We will take revenge
   on these fairy goddesses in Paradise
if through God's justice
   they become houris.

Sleep is his, his mind is his,
　　and nights
become his when your unfurled curls
　　drown his shoulders.

I step into the flower garden
　　and, hearing me weep,
a school of nightingales
　　become poets reciting ghazals.

Why are glances
　　slashing my heart, O Lord?
When bad luck comes
　　each glance is an eyelash.

I try to stop them,
　　but they bubble up in my chest.
Each sigh becomes
　　a stitch in my torn collar.

Even if I go there,
　　how can I answer her insults?
I spend what prayers
　　come to mind on her doorkeeper.

Wine gives life
　　to whoever holds the goblet,
all his palm lines
　　becoming life veins.

We are monotheists
　　and our sect discards rituals.
When creeds are erased,
　　we become one faith.

When pain stuns you,
    pain wanes.
I suffer until
    it becomes easy.

O people of the world, watch out!
    If Ghalib keeps weeping
your town will become
    a wilderness.

(Ghazal 111)

Handful of Dust

When my heart sees a hot scene,
    jealousy makes it icy.
My wince cracks wide open
    with what the eye sees.

The joy of sin should be strong
    as my heart hunger.
My hemline soaks up
    seven high seas.

Each handful of dust in the garden
    croons like a turtledove,
because she's tall as a cypress,
    and her strut's a mite obscene.

(Ghazal 117)

Dust

The joys of the world
  in my eyes are dust.
The liver holds liver blood and nothing
  besides dust.

Maybe when I wind up dust,
  the wind will fly me away.
Despite wing fervor and force in a feather,
  my flight is dust.

Who is coming,
  with marks of paradise?
The road is a glory of roses,
  with no sign of dust.

Should I pity myself
  since she did not?
The dead end feeling of my deadened feelings
  has not died to dust.

Rose glory dreams
  have spoiled the drinkers' wine.
The tavern's doors and walls
  are dry as dust.

I am shamed
  by the wrecking ball of passion.
What is built inside this house?
  Pipedreams rise from dust.

Asad! Your verse
  is trivial.
In the art of recitation here is the profit:
  a sky of dust.

(Ghazal 114)

Why Sing the Blues?

Why sing the blues?
   You gave your heart away.
No heart in your chest?
   Why have a tongue in your mouth?

She will not stop being herself.
   Why should I stop being proud?
Why be soft headed and ask,
   "Why are you hard headed with me?"

Your empathy busts me.
   Let this love combust and burn!
You cannot take the oven of grief.
   Why dish my secrets to you?

What are faith and passion
   if they make me smash my head with a stone?
Stone Heart, why imagine
   I will use your door stone?

I am in this cage, but it is fine
   to tell me garden news.
Why would yesterday's lightning
   fall on my nest?

You can say,
   "You are not in my heart,"
but since my heart holds only you,
   why hide from my eyes?

Why complain that your heart attracts.
   Whose fault is that?
Why be a magnet
   if you do not want to attract?

The disaster you are
    can wreck a man's house.
Why worry about malevolent sky?
    Your friendship is bad enough.

If this is testing,
    what do you call torture?
Since you belong to my enemy,
    why test me?

You say, "Why should I feel ashamed
    to meet the other man?"
You are right. It is true.
    Why should you be?

You want this kind of taunt to work,
    Ghalib?
But if you call her unkind.
    why should she be kind to you?

(Ghazal 126)

Why?

Why shouldn't it brim with pain,
    this heart neither stone nor brick?
Why do people mock me
    if I weep a thousand times?

This is no temple, no harem,
    not a door, not even a mosque.
Why do strangers ask me to clear out
    when I'm sitting by the road?

Illuminating heart, each afternoon you rise,
    a sun aflame.
Why hide your face
    when you are the burning spectacle?

Your love-glance daggers are fatal,
    your flirtation arrows endless.
Why look in the mirror
    and confront that deadly face?

We are sentenced to life
    and to a chain of sorrows,
so why seek to be free of grief
    before you die?

Beautiful, you know you are, so do not play.
    Spare me that shame.
Why do you test strangers
    when you're self-possessed?

There you are, proud and haughty.
    Here I am in a veil of modesty.
Why invite me to a gathering,
    when you will not meet me on the path?

Yes, she doesn't fear God.
    Let her be unfaithful.
If you adore faith and heart,
    why then, do not enter her alley.

When ramshackle Ghalib is dead,
    nobody will stop work.
Why weep and bawl,
    why howl and wail?

(Ghazal 115)

What We Say

When I say "I feel this way,"
   you say, "Say what you mean."
Say now, when you say that,
   what could anyone say?

Do not taunt me by saying again,
   "So I'm just a tyrant?"
because my habit is to say,
   "Whatever you say, dear."

Sure, it is a lancet,
   but when it lances the heart,
your loving glance,
   why wouldn't I say, "I love it"?

This arrowhead wound
   gives no relief.
I say, "I need a sword to slash
   my heart with joy."

If you have an enemy,
   do not be her enemy.
When she curses you,
   do not say a word.

At times we write the truth
   of our soul-wasting disease.
At times we say,
   "The trouble is, this medicine's no good."

Sometimes we complain
   of the heavy descent of grief.
Sometimes we say a parable
   of patience sprinting away.

If no life remains,
    pay your murderer the blood money.
If your tongue is sliced off,
    say, "Blessings!" to the knife.

If your love idol feels no love, fine!
    After all, she is an idol.
Say, "Look how she sways!
    Oh, her narcotic style!"

If the springtime has no time, fine!
    It is spring, after all.
Say, "How lusty the garden is!
    Oh, the lushness in the air."

Now that your ship
    has entered the dock, Ghalib,
What's the point of saying,
    "Lord, the captain was bitter cruel."

(Ghazal 209)

Glances Lined with Kohl

When you are silent, charm
  flirts on your face.
Heart glances lined with kohl
  dart from your face.

A private place
  so tight it squeezes out dew.
A gust pierces the folds of a bud, then
  spurts to the face.

Do not ask the lover's chest,
  "Was the sword glance sharp?"
The door is wounded and sighs
  burst from its face.

(Ghazal 227)

Kohl for the Eyes

I am kohl for the eyes, given free
    but with a fine to face.
What you owe me
    will eyeline your face.

Tyrant, give me
    permission to wail,
or the grief I veil
    will shine from your face.

(Ghazal 44)

Hennaed Feet

Desire complains
   at the heart's tight seal.
In the pearl curls
   a swirling high sea.

I know I won't see you
   answer my letters,
yet wear out my pen,
   writing to see.

Spring is just henna
   on autumn's feet.
The world's joy
   is the heart blight in me.

I miss you so much
   I can't stroll through gardens
without holding my nose
   if a rose smiles at me.

I'm so desperate
   for your beauty,
every follicle seeks
   to be an eye that sees.

I gave my heart
   before you flirted,
before beauty claimed
   its right to me.

Do not say weeping
   grows as the heart longs.
My eyes ebb and flood
   like the sea.

When I look up to Heaven,
  I remember you. Asad!
You act like God,
  all ire, no mercy.

(Ghazal 27)

I Am Human, After All

Am I not fallen
   at your door?
Throw dust on this life!
   I'm not made of stone.

Why wouldn't the always-gyring heart
   be anxious?
I am human, after all,
   not a cup or a sea.

O Lord, why do these times
   try to erase me?
I am a word not carved
   on the tablet of the world.

There must be a limit
   to this torture.
I am a sinner after all,
   not an infidel.

Why do you not
   think me precious?
Am I not a ruby, an emerald,
   gold, a pearl?

Why keep your footprints
   so far from my eyes?
I am sun and moon;
   my position is not less.

Why do you forbid me
   to kiss your footsteps?
Am I not even equal
   to the sky, to you?

Ghalib you are a pensioner,
   so bless the Shah.
The days are gone when you could say,
   "I'm not a servant."

(Ghazal 110)

The Stare

She's left and I stare
  at the walls, the door.
Sometimes I stare at the wind,
  sometimes at her messenger.

When she enters my home
  it is a miracle of God.
At times I stare at her,
  at time stare at my home.

Let no evil eye touch
  her hands and shoulders.
Why do these people stare
  at my liver wound?

Why should I care about
  the jewels studding your cap?
I stare at how high they ride, those lucky
  rubies and diamonds.

(Ghazal 106)

Rupture

What cruelty was left
    when she left off cruelty?
"What? You think I'd show
    my face to you?"

The seven heavens
    are spinning day and night.
What good is worrying?
    What happens, happens.

Rupture with me,
    and I will hear it as rapture.
What could trick me,
    since nothing exists?

Why did you walk off
    with the messenger?
What to do?
    How can I send my letter? Oh, lord!

Let waves of blood
    wash overhead.
What could make me leave
    my lover's doorstep?

All my life I've watched the road
    for death to show.
What could I show,
    now that I am dead?

They ask me,
    who is this man, Ghalib?
What should I say?
    Someone, please say.

(Ghazal 46)

The Face in the Mirror

The face in the mirror
   shocks her now,
this lady once so proud
   of not giving her heart.

Don't use those hands
   to strangle the messenger.
He's not to blame.
   Please, blame me!

(Ghazal 40)

More to Say

He gave her his heart. It is human.
   What more to say?
So what if he becomes a rival?
   There's more to say: He's a Messenger.

You are so stubborn.
   You will come for me, but not today.
I have such a problem with death.
   No more to say.

So stubborn: you will not come today,
   but you will not hesitate on my last day.
That's why I complain about fate.
   No more to say.

My rival eases on my beloved's street.
   He's there every day
till the street is my enemy's house.
   What more is there to say?

Her side-long glances
   have bewitched me.
Amazing! She knows everything
   without saying a thing.

In the bazaar, she asks me,
   "Are you well?"
"Well," I say, "we're standing in the street.
   What can I say?"

You do not consider how loyalty
   ties like a thread tip.
There's something in our hands,
   but can you say what?

When I question, she insists—passionately.
    Why fight her?
I gaze away from answers.
    What more to say?

My eloquence is punished—with jealousy.
    What can be done?
My craft is rewarded—with tyranny.
    What can one say?

She says,
    "Ghalib is not too bad,
except his brain is scrambled.
    What's there to say?"

(Ghazal 201)

Some Life

If for one more day
  I have some life,
In my life,
  I will do some more.

Hellfire has
  no such heat;
the heat of hidden grief
  is something worse.

How often
  I've heard her complain,
but her hammer-headedness
  today is something else!

The messenger hands the letter,
  then eyes her mouth
for some message
  to come from her tongue.

So often stars
  slice off our lives,
but this galactic calamity
  is something else.

Ghalib, you've seen
  every disaster.
There is something more:
  the deathblow.

(Ghazal 160)

When the Dead Rise

The cradle rocks
    when Jesus moves his lips.
Doomsday is the stone dream
    of those slain by an idol's ruby lips.

(Ghazal 222)

A Footprint in Paradise

The world sees
   your embossed footprint
in flowerbeds and flowerbeds
   we see as paradise.

The heart made sick by the mole
   at the edge of her lip
sees the heart's blackness
   as a stroll through blankness.

He's one Adam tall;
   she's a cypress tree, so tall
he sees her dwarf
   the tantrum of Doomsday.

The mirror takes you in,
   a spectacle
I see with
   so much longing.

Follow the steam wisping
   from the scar in my heart
and you will see footprints
   of the prowler in the night.

Disguise yourself
   as a fakir, Ghalib,
and you will see a spectacle
   —what generous people give.

(Ghazal 96)

Be Generous

Be generous. Call me sometime
    when you can squeeze in the time.
I am not like gone time
    that will not repeat sometime.

A word is not a head
    too heavy to lift.
My rival taunts. I do not complain.
    I just feel so weak sometimes.

Tyrant! I can't even find poison.
    Anyway,
how could I eat it when I can't swallow
    us never again meeting sometime?

(Ghazal 89)

Veil

We do not even tolerate
  our own envy.
We'd rather die,
  since needing her is vile.

Behind the veiling screen,
  she meets him secretly.
Outside, her veil is
  that she does not wear her veil.

If you revile Ghalib,
  his lustful rival
will lose hope.
  Do not. That's just evil.

(Ghazal 198)

What?

What happened to you,
   naïve heart?
What panacea
   for my pain at last?

I am agog
   and she is glum.
What is happening?
   Oh, Lord.

I too keep a tongue
   in my mouth.
What is my intent?
   I wish you'd ask.

Since nothing exists
   without You,
what is this hulabaloo,
   Oh, Lord.

What is it
   with these fairy-faced people?
What is all this lust, flirtation,
   and sidelong glancing?

Why this coiling
   amber-scented hair?
What dark glance
   from your antimony eyes?

From where these blossoms
   and greenery?
What is wind?
   What are clouds?

I hope she
   will be faithful.
What is faithfulness?
   She doesn't know.

Yes! Do good, and good
   will come to you.
What else does the dervish
   murmur, after all?

I offer my life
   to you.
What is prayer?
   I do not know.

Ghalib is nothing.
   I admit that.
What is the harm,
   if you get him for free?

(Ghazal 162)

The Cure for Life

My sigh won't do a thing
    until this whole life unfurls at last.
But who can last till that day
    when you unsnarl your curls at last?

In the net of each wave
    a hundred crocodile mouths circle.
Let's watch until a raindrop
    turns into a pearl at last.

Love orders, Be patient.
    Desire says, I can't wait.
Before it turns to liver-blood,
    what colors will my heart swirl at last?

We agreed
    you won't neglect me,
but I will turn to dust waiting
    before you get the word at last.

From a sunray
    the dew learns oblivion
just as I exist, until
    your flirting glance is hurled at last.

Reckless one!
    Long life is a fast glance.
The party's warmth
    is a dancing spark that lulls at last.

Life is grief, Asad.
    The cure for life is death.
The candle fevers in all colors
    till dawn recurs at last.

(Ghazal 78)

Infected by Love

I am a caregiver
    to one infected by love.
What to do with a Messiah
    who can't even heal himself?

(Ghazal 55)

No Medicine

My pain comes
    with no debt to medicine,
but I come out well
    even if I do not get well.

Why do you gather
    all my rivals?
I do not complain
    at the spectacle to come.

Where can I go
    to test my luck
if you will not come
    to test your dagger on me?

How much sugar
    is in your lips?
Even when you nag, my rival comes away
    with a sweet taste.

Hot news:
    my lover approaches.
On this of all days, I can't come
    on a rag in my house!

Nimrod was godlike
    but what good is that?
My devotion to you comes
    with no reward.

I give back my life
    that was given to me,
but fail to come through
    on my debts.

The wound heals,
   but the blood isn't stanched.
If I stop working,
   my work will not come again.

Are you mugging me,
   or is this a heart-tease?
Heart-teaser, come on!
   You flee, carrying my heart.

Read something!
   The people are babbling
because Ghalib hasn't come
   to recite his ghazals.

(Ghazal 26)

Where Is My Heart?

You say, "If I find your heart
    lying around, I'm keeping it."
Where is my heart?
    How can it be lost, since I've found you?

In love my spirit found
    the tang of life,
found the cure for pain
    in pain with no cure.

My faithful heart
    is my enemy's friend.
I find my "Ah!" has no effect.
    No one hears me keening.

Her simplicity is a skill;
    her indifference has a plan.
It tried my courage, but I found
    beauty in her apathy.

The bud began to bud again today,
    and I found
my heart transformed to blood.
    I found it lost.

I do not know my heart,
    except in this:
how often I hunted it,
    how often you found it.

After the mullah salts my wound
    with brackish words
I ask him, "Did you find it tasty?
    I did."

(Ghazal 4)

Famine

What help will my friends be
    while I suffer?
And what use? My nails will grow long
    before this wound scabs!

How is your infinite dispassion,
    O servant of Allah?
I say my heart hurts
    and you say, "What?"

The honorable mullah walks in.
    My eyes and heart are his carpet.
Could someone explain to me
    what he's trying to explain?

Today I go there
    wearing a sword and death shroud.
What excuse can she have
    for not killing me this time?

If the mullah imprisons me,
    so be it!
What? Will that make me kick
    my addiction to lunatic love?

Your curly hair enslaves me.
    Why should I escape such chains?
What prison cell could trouble me
    when love is my prison?

Asad! I'm famished for love-grief,
    but this town is in famine.
Of course, I'd love to live in Delhi.
    But what would I eat there?

(*Ghazal 19*)

A Woundgift

A woundgift, a diamondgift,
    a liverscar offering.
Kudos, Asad! Someone's arrived
    to feel your lifepain, eat your grief.

(Ghazal 2)

Who Cares?

If you aren't satisfied
    with my death, who cares?
Even if I have to pass
    more tests, who cares?

Desire to see you
    is a thorn that pricks.
If desire picks no flowers
    in the garden of rest, who cares?

Wine worshippers drink
    straight from the cask,
so if the Cupbearer is not among
    the guests, who cares?

The breath of Qais is the eye-lamp
    of the desert.
Laila's black tent has no candle,
    but do not fret. Who cares?

A house needs some excitement,
    to have life,
if not happy music,
    dirges instead. Who cares?

I do not want praise,
    do not care for reward.
If my poetry has
    no depth, who cares?

To be with a beauty
    is a lucky strike.
Ghalib, if you die before
    your death, who cares?

(Ghazal 175)

Heartgrief School

No one but Qais
    could face it:
the desert narrowed
    to a jealous eye.

Frenzy was a black scab
    on my heart,
but the scar
    was just a smoke smudge.

In dream your thoughts
    have business with you.
Your eyes open to
    nothing won, nothing lost.

I'm still a student
    at heartgrief school.
I've learned qwat gang is what's gone
    and qwat wes is what was.

The shroud cloaked
    my naked body's scars.
In any other clothes,
    I would disgrace this life.

Asad! Kohkaan couldn't kill himself
    without a pickaxe;
he was brain-stoned,
    drunk with canons and customs.

(Ghazal 3)

The Desert Sea

Without me weeping,
   my house would be bleak inside.
The sea would be a desert
   if weren't sea inside.

Why should I complain
   about my griefstruck infidel heart?
If it weren't full of grief,
   anxiety could squeeze inside.

If only Rizwan, sentry of Paradise,
   kept my lover's gate!
After this life of abstinence
   he might let me free inside.

(Ghazal 31)

Wasteland

Again I recall
    her tear-glazed gaze.
My heart and liver call out,
    thirsting for my lover.

Doomsday had not yet
    paused for breath
when I recalled
    the time you left.

Oh, Desire,
    your simplicity
makes me recall
    my lover's witching glance.

Excuse my longings,
    O thirsty heart.
When I call out,
    I recall my lover.

Life might have passed
    so easily.
Why did I recall
    the path you walked?

What a fight I will have
    with the angel Rizwan,
in Paradise
    if I recall your house.

How can I get the courage
    to beg?
Recalling my lover,
    I'm tired of my heart.

Once again, my thoughts
    wander your alleys.
Maybe I can call back
    my lost heart.

My wasteland
    is such a wasteland
that seeing the desert,
    I recall home.

Asad! Like a child
    I heft a stone
to attack Majnun
    —then recall my senses.

(Ghazal 35)

The Traveler

Ghalib, the walls and doors
   are sprouting green
while I'm off in the wasteland,
   my home becoming spring.

(Ghazal 156)

Call Down Lightning

All I do is laze about;
    they're right to sneer at me.
In my hometown,
    dawn's teeth leer at me.

My soul hunts a singer
    with fiery breath
whose voice calls lightning
    down to sear me.

I wander the delirious valley
    of my thoughts
'til no desire to return
    appears to me.

You unveil lewdly
    in the garden.
I blush when roses
    scent the air near me.

How could my secret heart
    be known?
My own poems
    smear me.

(Ghazal 149)

Lunatic Beggar

Asad! I am a lunatic beggar,
   drifting headless, heedless.
The deer's eyelashes
   are combs that claw my back.

(Ghazal 23)

Madness of the Night of Separation

With every step
   the goal recedes from me.
At my own pace
   the desert flees from me.

A vision thread
   stitches my eyelashes shut.
Not reading titles on the binding
   agrees with me.

My heart flames wildly
   in this desolate night.
Like smoke my shadow
   twirls free from me.

May idols not teach lovers
   this simple thing: grief.
The mirror-chamber
   reflects emptily: me.

My blisters decorate
   the desert of my lunacy:
a luminous string of pearls
   leaks from me.

Non-self is the bedspread
   of my leisure.
My night chamber swells
   with shadowings of me.

When your lustful gaze
   slices through my neck,
I am a trimmed candle
   and glances scatter free of me.

O helplessness!
    O madness of the night of separation!
In the apocalyptic sun,
    my shadow is concealed from me.

You make the goblet
    spin through a hundred colors,
the mirror of a single astounded eye
    dreams in me.

Asad! A flame drips
    from my burning eye
till garden rags and shavings
    are fire seeds to me.

(Ghazal 190)

Blood-Filled Eyes

Even in silence my lover's eyes
    spoke a song.
The kohl around her eyes was a flaming
    smoking song.

On their bodies, lovers played music
    of an atonal star.
Planets revolved and sang like lovers
    a broken song.

See the power
    of Majnun's blood-filled eyes:
in the wasteland a miracle of roses
    awoke with song.

(Ghazal 147)

A Rose in the Dirt

My pain made you
    restless, O! O!
Brute! Where is your
    indifference now? O! O!

If your heart could not stomach
    my sorrow-storm,
then why did you drink
    my despair, O! O!

Why did you think
    to soften my pain?
Friendship to me made you
    your enemy, O! O!

You said you'd entwine yourself
    with me for life.
but life frays
    and unravels. O! O!

This water-and-air life
    is toxic to me
because it was unhealthy
    for you. O! O!

What happened to the rose's
    pride in blooming?
Red flowers embroider
    your clay now, O! O!

Shame drove you to hide
    in a veil of dirt.
The veil of love
    has been torn. O! O!

When love's fame
 blended into dirt,
the way of love
 left the planet. O! O!

Your sword-wielding hand
 slowly weakened
till not even one wound
 sliced my heart. O! O!

How can I survive
 black nights of the rainy season
with eyes so used
 to counting stars? O! O!

The ear cut off from the message,
 the eye blinded to miracle,
the heart made single,
 and now this hopelessness. O! O!

Love had not yet taken
 the color of madness, Ghalib.
What remained in my heart?
 A taste for wretchedness. O! O!

(Ghazal 139)

Give Me Lunacy, at Least

Love, I can't own you,
    but give me lunacy, at least.
Let my last lunacy be your
    legacy, at least.

Do not cut
    all ties with me.
Let me hate you and you
    hate me, at least.

What shame in me
    being with you?
If not in public, see me
    privately, at least.

Go ahead,
    believe he loves you.
I'm not my own
    enemy, at least.

From my being should be
    whatever should be:
if not mindfully, then
    mindlessly, at least.

Though life is
    fast lightning,
there's time for my heart
    to drain free, at least.

It is not like
    I'm giving up faith.
If love fails, I will take
    calamity, at least.

Give me a shred,
    O unjust sky.
Let me sigh
    resentfully, at least.

I must resign myself
    and make it a habit.
You're stingy
    naturally, at least.

Asad! Your lover
    keeps teasing you.
If she will not bed you, then want her
    urgently, at least.

(Ghazal 148)

How Tight Is the World?

How tight is the world
   of we the oppressed?
The universe
   is one ant egg.

Your zest is the engine
   of the cosmos.
A sunray is the flash of life
   in a sand grain.

This redness comes
   from a stone smack.
Yet that cretin suspects
   there is wine in my glass.

She heats the chest
   of those who lust.
Why wouldn't she like it?
   It is like a cool house.

So you did not kiss the stranger?
   Bravo!
Enough. Shut up.
   There is a tongue in my mouth, too.

When he sits in the shade
   of his lover's wall
he is the Raja
   of Hindustan.

Grief effaced
   even my belief in life.
Whom should I tell:
   This scar is my liver's last trace.

Ghalib, these days
    your belief in faith is so great,
that you find joy in this:
    She is ungrateful.

                                        (Ghazal 138)

The Tulip

In the field of being, the tulip is
    a brooding wound.
Lightning striking is balm for the gardener's
    bloody wound.

The bud feels secure
    until it blooms.
Despite its closed heart, the rose's dream
    is a budding wound.

How can I bear this wearing grief
    when I am weak,
straw in the flame's teeth, a man knuckling under,
    mud in my wound.

(Ghazal 155)

Dew on a Red Tulip

Dew blooms on a red tulip
   for a reason:
to make a charred heart ashamed
   of going numb.

Twitching with lust to see her,
   my heart hemorrhages
and henna-stains the mirror
   in a drunken idol's palm.

Flame doesn't burn
   like the lust for flame.
How my heart is charred
   by her frigid heart!

Your image flirts
   with multifoliate delight.
The mirror is an open
   rose bloom embrace.

The dove is a froth of ash,
   the nightingale a jail of color.
O keening voice,
   what is this burnt liver mark?

Your nature numbs
   the wild heart.
A passionless lover
   is strange disaster.

Love arrested me.
   My promise is a shackle.
My hand will not stray
   with this boulder on it.

I see dead martyrs
    pictured
in the mirror
    of your vicious sword.

Sun who lights the world,
    warm me too.
A strange time is on me
    like a shadowfall.

Give me justice.
    There are sins I didn't commit.
But Lord is there retribution
    for those I did!

People do not care for you.
    Do not lose heart, Ghalib.
If you have no one, my dear,
    there is still God.

(*Ghazal 230*)

Nothing Is What Breathes from Me

For once, she thinks
    of acting sweet to me,
then shies in shame
    of how she's treated me.

O Lord! The heart repels
    when it is attracted,
for when I pull at her
    she flees from me.

She's curt with me
    for blathering of love too long
Long story short: it is like her courier
    has fleas 'round me.

There's wariness in her;
    there's weakness here.
She asks nothing, and nothing
    is what breathes from me.

End of the world! It is hopeless.
    I have to get a grip.
The hemline of the thought of her
    slips free from me.

My point is,
    even if I'm gazing too,
if others see her, then
    the scene's obscene to me.

My feet took the first wound
    in the love battle.
I can't run off, but staying's
    misery for me.

Ghalib, it is Doomsday!
　　She is traveling with that faker.
Kaafir woman, do not expect
　　"Godspeed" from me.

(Ghazal 205)

Nothing

Before being there was God.
   If nothing were, God still would be.
Being drowns me.
   What matter if I have no being?

Brain-numbed from grief,
   I'm decapitated, yet I feel nothing.
I will rest my head on my knees,
   if it is still attached to me.

It has been eons since Ghalib died.
   But it is remembered
how he asked,
   "What would have been if it had been?"

(Ghazal 32)

No One

Let me live somewhere
   in brotherhood with no one,
speaking and being
   understood by no one.

I'd like to build a door-less,
   wall-less house
with no guard, here in the
   neighborhood of no one.

Then when I fall sick
   no one will be my healer.
My dirge will be sung the way
   it should—by no one.

(Ghazal 127)

Notes on the Poems

Page 45, Stanza 4: Hazra Khizr is considered in the Islamic tradition to be an immortal prophet. He was Alexander the Great's guide to the fountain of eternal life, but abandoned Alexander along the way and he drank of the water of life himself.

Page 47: This ghazal is a bit unusual, in that it has no repeated words, just end-rhymes. Khizr, in line 2, is considered in the Islamic tradition to be an immortal prophet, because he drank of the water of life.

Page 48: Sharia is the Arabic term for Islamic religious law. Khizr was Alexander the Great's guide to the fountain of eternal life, but abandoned Alexander along the way and took life everlasting for himself.

Page 53, Stanza 5: The Ka'aba is the house of Allah for Muslims, the most holy temple in Mecca.

Page 56, Stanza 3: The Ka'aba is the most holy temple in Mecca.

Page 57: In the third stanza, the Urdu uses a construction that collapses two words into one (Qiblah-goal and humble-gaze). Qiblah means the direction of Ka'aba (the holy temple in Mecca), the direction in which Muslims are to pray five times a day. However, in this ironic verse, the Ka'aba's curtains turn out to be the curtains of an elephant litter in which the lover is riding.

Page 58, Stanza 3: A more literal reading of the lines would be something like, "The world becomes dark / again in the cord-holding court-officer of her curls," but *andher* means both darkness and tyranny, and *sarishtah-daar* means a court officer, court petitioner, or court recorder, but *sarishtah* means rope or cord, as well as customs or ceremonies. Thus, there is a sense that the curled/corded hair is both the court officer and the rope that ties the lover up and turns his world to dark tyranny, and we tried to bring those puns to the surface. At first we played with the idea of rending the line, "Court-recorder, record how the world / is bound in darkness by her corded hair," but felt that it made the line too ornate and complicated.

Page 59, Stanza 6: The Ka'aba is the most holy temple in Mecca, and the

Well of Zamzam is said to have been revealed to Hagar, the wife of Abraham, when their son, Ishmael was weeping with thirst and kicking the earth. It is in Mecca, near the Ka'aba, and is a place of pilgrimage for millions who come to drink its water.

Page 62, Stanza 1: The Cupbearer refers to the bearer of love, an intoxicating connection. Allegorically, drinking wine produces love for Allah, and thus the cupbearer is sometimes seen as Muhammad.

Page 65, Stanzas 1 and 3: The wine duck is a goblet in the form of a duck.

The Huma is a Persian mythological bird whose shadow is supposed to bring great good fortune. If the bird lands on your head, you are destined to become King, or perhaps to develop your mind to a king-like, enlightened state.

Page 68: Stanzas 2 and 6: The lines in the mirror are like poetic gems or polished lines of poetry, but he's presenting them as thorns because he's breaking poetic convention by using so many combined-word constructions in a row.

The salamander is a mythical lizard who is born from fire.

Page 71: Stanza 2: Jamshid, the mythical 4th king of Persia, was a great ruler who possessed a divine radiance (farr) and wisdom. He was supposed to have possessed a magical scrying cup in which he could see all the seven heavens of the universe. The world was reflected in the cup, and the cup gave its owner power to rule well and with knowledge. Although kingdoms pass down along with seals of authority, wisdom is to be found in the wineglass, which might not be passed down from ruler to ruler. Even Jamshid fell from grace because of his pride in his accomplishment, and lost his divine farr and was murdered by an usurper, the dragon-king Zahhak.

Page 73, Stanza 1: For Jamshid, see note to "The Betel Nut."

Page 74: In this poem, there is no repeating word or phrase, just a repeating sound within words (rhyme), so we are repeating the "ur" sound in our version.

Page 76: This ghazal is unusual in that there is no repeating phrase.

Page 78: This ghazal originally had 12 verses, but Ghalib cut it down to eight for publication. The following verse was originally the 11th couplet in the poem.

> Every now and then I am a parrot
>   with sugared speech, but
> ah! Mirror face, you no longer remain
>   facing off with me.

In stanza 2, the word we have translated as "congregation" could mean a gathering of a group of friends, but in the Sufi tradition the term refers to a spiritual gathering of saints and prophets.

Page 83, Stanza 3: The three stars in the handle of the Great Dipper are known in Arab and Persian culture as the Daughters of the Dead, or Daughters of the Bier, because they resemble pall bearers walking before a coffin.

Stanza 4: The Biblical/Quranic character of the prophet Joseph (Yusef) was a figure of extraordinary beauty, known by the epithet "The Moon of Canaan." In Egypt, he was sold as a slave to Potiphar (or Kitfir, in the Quran), whose wife was the great beauty Zulaikha. Zulaikha tried her best to tempt Joseph with her charms, but he resisted. Zulaikha chased after Joseph and tore his shirt, at which point her husband walked in, and the spurned Zulaikha accused Joseph of the crime which he had resisted, causing Joseph to be thrown in prison. The women of the city scorned Zulaikha for being smitten with Joseph, but Zulaikha gave 100 of the women lemons and knives, and sent for Joseph, saying, "When you see Joseph, peel the lemons with the knives." But upon seeing his great beauty, the women were so thunderstruck that they cut their own fingers instead. Later, after the death of Potiphar, Joseph married Zulaikha.

Page 102: The idea is that Ghalib has sent the lady a message that has made her so mad she wants to "kill the messenger," so to speak. Ghalib loves her so much that he shouts out that the fault is all his, preferring she strangle him with her lovely hands than that she touch another man.

Page 109: In verse two, the word "pardah" is used three times: first to indicate the cloth that separates women from men in Muslim households; second to indicate that she's hiding something; third to indicate that she's not wearing the "pardah" or veil that women wear in public and with men who might be considered possible mates. Thus, by not wearing the veil in public, she is veiling her true relationship with him—that she meets him behind the cloth in the household.

Page 112, Stanza 2: According to Indian folklore, a raindrop that reaches the sea unscathed and is swallowed by an oyster will become a pearl. Thus the dangers of the wave—the net, the crocodile mouths—are dangers that hinder the transformation of the drop (the self) into something wonderful.

Page 114, Stanza 6: Nimrod (Namrud) was a king of Mesopotamia who decreed that all infant boys be put to death because he dreamed that a child to be born would be a great prophet, more powerful than he was. The child, Abraham, survives and is forced by the king to perform miracles, and burned alive for a week when he declares there is only one God, Nimrod himself desiring to be worshiped as a god. However, Abraham survives the flames, and is joined by Sarah, Nimrod's daughter in the flames, who becomes his wife. Nimrod attacks with his army but God kills Nimrod and his men with a great swarm of mosquitoes.

Page 116, Stanza 7: The mullah/Advisor is a preacher who pops up in a number of Ghalib poems, usually offering moralistic but unwelcome advice to the passionate speaker.

Page 118: Implicitly, the visitor who sympathizes with Asad (another name for Ghalib) is also the one who wounds him. However, the lover wants the wound of love, considers it a gift, an offering. It is precious to him as a diamond, though sharp diamonds slice the internal organs if swallowed.

Page 119, Stanza 4: For Qais and Laila, the great Arabic lovers, see note to "Heartgrief School."

Page 120, Stanza 1: Qais is another name for the great Arab lover, Majnun, who went crazy for the love of Laila when her father wouldn't let them marry, and wandered the deserts in lunacy.

Stanza 4 provided a fascinating translation problem. In the Urdu, the line reads, "I've learned that went went and was was," but the interesting thing is that Ghalib uses the Persian for the first "gone" and the Urdu for the second "gone," and the same thing with the verb "was." Ghalib wrote both in Persian (the language of the Mughal court) and Urdu (the vernacular language), and he is probably doing a wordplay upon the fact that Urdu is a language that derived from the joining of Persian with Hindustani, among other influences (such as Sanskrit, Arabic, Turkic, Punjabi and English). Thus, one meaning of the line is that words that were Persian have become Urdu. Another meaning of the line is that heartbreak school teaches that what's gone is gone. In seeking a parallel linguistic play, we've substituted in the Middle English for "gone" and "was."

Stanza 6 refers to Kohkaan, literally "Mountain-Cutter," another term for the famous Persian lover, Farhaad. Kohkaan was a stone mason who fell in love with a princess, Shirin. The Shah told him he could marry the princess if does what the Shah thinks is impossible: to cut a grand canal through a mountain. But Kohkaan works hard for years and accomplishes the task, so the Shah plays a trick on him, and sends word that in the meantime Shirin has died. In his grief, Kohkaan stabs himself in the head with his spade, and his blood runs in the canal. When Shirin hears of his death, she goes to the same spot and kills herself in the same way, so that their blood runs together in the canal. In this verse, Ghalib is poking fun at him for needing a blade to kill himself instead of just dying of grief from heartbreak, and perhaps for following the directives of the Shah instead of just eloping with his love

Page 122, Stanza 6: Rizwan is the angel who serves as the gatekeeper of the Islamic Paradise. Ghalib is either saying he'll have to fight Rizwan to leave Paradise and go to her house, or that he'll disagree about whether her house is better than Paradise.

Page 123: In the third stanza, Majnun is another name for Qais, the great lover of the Islamic tradition (see note for Ghazal 3). Majnun was in one version of the story sentenced to be stoned to death for killing Laila's brother

Tabrez for refusing to allow the lovers to marry. Perhaps Ghalib is like a village child throwing stones at the madman because he has suffered so much for emulating the great lunatic lover, but then he is called back to his senses—which ironically means he goes back to being mad with love.

Page 127: In stanza 2, we have reversed the order of lines 3 and 4, so as to maintain the repeated word and convey the full meaning.

The Translators

Tony Barnstone is Professor of English and Environment Studies at Whittier College and the author of twenty-one books, a creativity tool titled *The Radiant Tarot: Pathway to Creativity,* and and a music CD. He has served as the Visiting Distinguished Professor in Creative Writing in the MFA Program at Bowling Green State University and as the Visiting Professor of Translation in the Ph.D. Program at the University of California, Irvine. He has a Masters in English and Creative Writing and Ph.D. in English Literature from the University of California at Berkeley.

In addition to *Pulp Sonnets,* his books of poetry include *Beast in the Apartment; Tongue of War: From Pearl Harbor to Nagasaki,* winner of the John Ciardi Prize in Poetry; *The Golem of Los Angeles,* which won the Poets Prize and the Benjamin Saltman Award in Poetry; *Sad Jazz: Sonnets*; and *Impure: Poems by Tony Barnstone,* and a chapbook of poems titled *Naked Magic* (Main Street Rag).

He is also a co-translator of Chinese poetry and literary prose and an editor of literary textbooks. His books in these areas include *Mother Is a Bird: Sonnets of Yi Poet; Chinese Erotic Poetry; The Anchor Book of Chinese Poetry; Out of the Howling Storm: The New Chinese Poetry; Laughing Lost in the Mountains: Poems of Wang Wei; The Art of Writing: Teachings of the Chinese Masters;* and the textbooks *Literatures of Asia, Africa and Latin America, Literatures of Asia,* and *Literatures of the Middle East.*

His bilingual Spanish/English selected poems, *Buda en Llamas: Antología poética (1999-2012)* appeared in 2014. He has also co-edited the anthologies *Republic of Apples, Democracy of Oranges: New Eco-Poetry from China and the United States, Dead and Undead Poems* and *Monster Verse.*

Among his awards are the Poets Prize, Grand Prize of the Strokestown International Poetry Festival, the Pushcart Prize in Poetry, fellowships from the National Endowment for the Arts, the National Endowment for the Humanities, and the California Arts Council, the Benjamin Saltman Award in Poetry and the John Ciardi Prize in Poetry. *Tokyo's Burning: World War II Songs,* his CD of folk rock/blues songs (in collaboration with singer-songwriters

Ariana Hall and John Clinebell, based upon *Tongue of War*) is available on Amazon.com, Rhapsody, and CD Baby.

His website is https://www.whittier.edu/academics/english/barnstone

Bilal Shaw is a Kashmiri-American computer scientist who completed his doctoral degree in quantum information science from the University of Southern California, and his undergraduate degree in mathematics from Whittier College. In addition to solving problems in quantum information science, he has contributed to DNA nanotechnology, software architecture design, and theoretical self-assembly. He currently lives in Los Angeles and works as the Director of Data Science for Neustar. He applies machine-learning to solve fraud, risk, and identity problems in the financial industry domain. With Tony Lee, Bilal has also recently completed a manuscript of the translations of Mir Taqi Mir's Urdu ghazals to English.